Caring

by Robin Doak

RAINTREE
STECK-VAUGHN
PUBLISHERS

A Harcourt Company

Austin   New York
www.raintreesteckvaughn.com

Published by Raintree Steck-Vaughn Publishers,
an imprint of Steck-Vaughn Company.

Library of Congress Cataloging-in-Publication Data is available upon request.

ISBN: 0-7398-5778-9

Printed and bound in China
1 2 3 4 5 6 7 8 9 10   05 04 03 02

A Creative Media Applications, Inc. Production

Photo Credits:
AP/Wide World Photographs: Cover
AP/Wide World Photographs: Pages 5, 7, 9, 10, 11, 14,
     17, 18, 22, 23, 24, 25, 27, 29
Kevin Hong/The (Aberdeen, Wash.) Daily World: Page 13
Jackie Moore/Pennies to Protect Police Dogs: Page 18
Tariq Khamisa Foundation: Page 26

Editor: Matt Levine
Indexer: Joan Verniero
Design and Production: Alan Barnett, Inc.
Photo Research: Yvette Reyes

Contents

"Always try to be a little kinder than necessary."
—James M. Barrie, author of *Peter Pan*

Caring. The word is simple enough to say and understand. But this small, simple word can make a huge change in the world around you. Without caring, the world would be a cold and lonely place.

People can show that they care for others in many different ways. Love, kindness, and **empathy** are all parts of caring. **Forgiveness** and gratitude show caring, too. Doing good deeds is another important way to show that you care. Even just taking a moment to listen to what someone has to say can be a caring thing to do.

Small Act of Caring

Pick up the phone and call a friend or relative. Ask that person about his or her day. Let your friend or relative know that you were thinking about him or her.

Mark Winter, left, and his wife, Ann, of Earlville, Iowa, listen as their grandson, Aaron O'Connor, 7, reads a book that he wrote about them. Every day, caring people make the world a better place.

Acts of caring help to make our world a kinder place. The tiniest gesture can change someone's day for the better. You have the power to improve your community by caring. Can you think of five small ways to make a difference?

Marian Wright Edelman: A Champion of Caring

Marian Wright Edelman has made the world a better place by caring. Edelman helps poor children and families in the United States. Edelman speaks out for these people because she cares. She works hard to get laws passed that aid Americans who are less fortunate than most.

Edelman was born in South Carolina in 1939. As a lawyer she began speaking out for those who could not always speak out for themselves. In the 1960s Edelman

Small Act of Caring

Write a letter to a caring person that you know or admire. For example, you might want to write to a community member, such as a firefighter or a police officer, who has shown caring in some way. You could also choose to write to a neighbor who has performed a good deed. Let the person know that you appreciate his or her efforts to make the world a kinder place. Tell that person how you have benefited from knowing him or her.

Marian Wright Edelman speaks at a rally in Washington, D.C. Edelman has spent most of her life helping children and families in the United States.

worked with Dr. Martin Luther King, Jr., to gain **civil rights** for blacks throughout the United States.

In 1973 Edelman founded the Children's Defense Fund (CDF). The CDF is a powerful voice for poor and homeless children. The group's mission is "to leave no child behind and to ensure every child a healthy start, a head start, a fair start, a safe start, and a moral start" in life.

Edelman feels that caring about others is an important part of living a good life. In her book *The Measure of Our Success: A Letter to My Children and Yours,* Edelman wrote, "Being considerate of others will take you and your children further in life than any college or professional degree."

Kids spend a lot of time in school. For many students, making their school community a caring one has become an important goal. Students across the nation have found many creative ways to show that they care.

Some students show that they care at school by becoming **peer mediators.** Peer mediators work with other students who are having problems or disagreements with one another. They are specially trained to help these students talk about and work out their problems.

Peer mediation can help schools become more caring communities. Students learn to listen to one another. They learn to express themselves. They also learn to forgive one another. Most importantly peer mediation helps children learn to solve their problems without violence.

Small Act of Caring

Talk to your principal about ways to reward small acts of kindness and caring in your school. One example is to give out caring stickers. Give special stickers to students who are seen doing something kind or caring.

Students in Seattle, Washington, peacefully march down Martin Luther King Way, calling for an end to violence in America. Nonviolent solutions are the best way to resolve conflicts.

Khalil Roberts, a peer mediator at Portland Middle School in Connecticut, thinks that mediation is a cool way to care. "Peer mediation lets kids know that there is always someone there to help them with their problems," he said.

Be a trendsetter! Did you know that small acts of caring can start a chain reaction? When you do something good for someone else, a number of things happen. First, you set an example for those around you. Also, the other person feels good. In turn, he or she might do something nice for someone else. Last, you get a good feeling from doing something nice for someone else.

Clayton Grinder, 10, of East Stroudsburg, Pennsylvania, rakes leaves in his grandparents' yard. A small act of caring can brighten someone's day.

There are many different ways to show caring for others. These students made sure that the new kid in their class did not sit alone at the lunch table.

Here are some things you can do to show that you care.

- Leave a note for your mom and dad, thanking them for being there.
- Help an elderly neighbor with a chore.
- Read a book to a small child.
- Put a quarter in a parking meter for someone whose time has expired.
- Smile and say hello to someone that you would not usually talk to.
- Share your lunch with someone who forgot his or hers.
- Carry groceries for someone.

Empathy is an important part of caring. Empathy is the ability to put yourself into another person's place. To show empathy, you must try to understand what others are thinking and feeling. When you put yourself in someone else's shoes, you can begin to understand how that person feels deep down inside.

How can you show empathy for a friend?

- Really listen to what your friend tells you. Do not interrupt or offer advice.

- Do not judge your friend. Instead, imagine yourself in his or her position.

- Let your friend know that his or her feelings are okay.

Empathy in Action

In Hoquiam, Washington, students showed empathy when a classmate was diagnosed with cancer in April 2001. Nick Kramzer was 11 years old when he learned that he had Hodgkin's disease. Hodgkin's disease is a type of cancer.

While he was receiving treatment for the disease, Nick's hair began to fall out in patches. Nick decided to shave his head. To show their support and caring for their friend, Nick's baseball teammates decided to do the same. One spring afternoon many of Nick's teammates shaved off their hair. Other community members also shaved their heads to show support for Nick.

The players who had their heads shaved were able to empathize with part of what Nick was going through. In addition they used the hair-shaving event to raise funds for Nick and his family. Nick's cancer treatment has been successful, and today he is on the road to recovery.

Nick Kramzer, second from left, poses with some of the kids who shaved their heads to show support for his battle against cancer. The children also raised funds to help Nick's family pay for his medical treatment.

How to Be a Good Friend

Caring people make good friends. You probably know that a true friend is someone that you can count on during both good and bad times. But did you know that treating your friends with caring and kindness is rewarding, too? When you show kindness to the people

From left, Felicia Bowman, 12, Rachael Jameson, 11, Randy Houtz, 11, Colton Dowman, 11, David Jameson, 11, and Will Hill, 6, eat frozen treats while hanging out on the porch.

Small Act of Caring

Use an index card and markers to make a "caring coupon" for your friend. A coupon might entitle the friend to a free ice cream cone, courtesy of you; five minutes of uninterrupted talk; or a chance to borrow a book or CD of choice from your personal library.

around you, they are more likely to give kindness and caring right back to you.

To be a good friend, keep in mind the Golden Rule: Treat others the way that you want to be treated. Also remember:

- **Be loyal.** Do not talk about your friend to others. Stand up for your friend when others are making fun of him or her.

- **Be dependable.** If you tell a friend that you are going to do something with him or her, do it. If you tell a friend that you are going to call at a certain time, carry through on your word.

- **Be a listener.** Be interested in what your friend has to say to you.

- **Be a communicator.** Let your friend know what is bothering you. Together, good friends can work through their problems.

When people you care about have problems, you want to help. You would like to fix what is wrong and make them feel better again. This is not usually possible, however. You cannot magically make people's problems go away.

So what can you do if someone that you care for is sad or upset? One of the best ways to show someone that you care is to just listen to what he or she has to say. Here is an example of someone who is listening carefully.

Makayla's friend Nicole is talking about a fight that she had with her sister. As Nicole talks, Makayla looks her in the eye and nods her head to show that she is listening

Talk It Out

Being a good listener is important—but remember that you need to talk, too! Putting your feelings into words allows people who care about you to help. Think of one or two people that you like to talk to. What makes them good listeners? How have they helped you work through your problems?

Sometimes the best thing to do for someone is to be a good listener.

closely. Makayla lets Nicole tell her story from start to finish without interrupting. She gives Nicole her undivided attention. When Nicole finishes her story, Makayla says, "I'm glad you told me that. If you need to talk again, I'm here for you." By being a good listener, Makayla shows Nicole how much she cares for her.

Senior citizens sometimes need a helping hand. There are some things that they may not be able to do as well as they once could. There are many ways that children can show seniors that they care. For example, a senior that you know might need some extra help around the house. In some communities around the nation, "rent-a-teen" programs offer free services to the elderly. Teens do

Clare Meadows, right, asks Dominic Penn, 13, a question as he helps her use a computer. When you help a senior citizen, you show caring and gain a new friend.

Great Ways to Care for a Special Senior

How can you shown seniors in your community that you care? Here are some suggestions.

- Offer to teach a senior how to use a computer and the Internet at the local library.
- Volunteer for an hour of yardwork each week. This might include weeding a garden, raking a lawn, or shoveling a sidewalk.
- Pay a surprise visit to your favorite senior.
- Read the daily newspaper to seniors at a nearby retirement home.

For more suggestions, call a local retirement home and ask how you can help.

chores that seniors may have difficulty with. For example, teens might volunteer to shop, do yardwork, or write letters for elderly people.

Sometimes senior citizens leave their homes to live in retirement communities. These seniors may miss their homes and become lonely. In Baltimore, Maryland, a group called Magic Me connects seniors in retirement communities with children aged 10 to 13. The children and seniors get together to dance, sing, read, and talk.

Another part of caring is **compassion.** Compassion is the desire to ease the sufferings and troubles of others. Some U.S. kids choose to show their compassion by helping animals in need. Some adopt animals that they find at shelters. Others donate their time or money to help protect wild animals and their natural environments.

Protecting Police Dogs

One person who has shown compassion and caring is Stacey Hillman of Casselberry, Florida. In 2000 the 10-year-old read a news story that talked about police dogs that were shot in the line of duty. Stacey decided that Florida's police dogs needed protection. She learned that special bulletproof vests were available, but these "K-9" vests were expensive. Many police departments could not afford them.

Small Act of Caring

Call your local animal shelter and see how you can help. You may wish to create a poster or flyer with pictures of animals that are available for adoption.

Stacey Hillman and friends. Stacey helped raise money to protect Florida police dogs. She wanted all police dogs in her area to have bulletproof vests.

Stacey took action. She founded the nonprofit group Pennies to Protect Police Dogs and began raising money. She started by asking people to fill jars with their extra change. Her goal was to buy a special bulletproof vest for every police dog in her area.

Since March 2000 Stacey has raised $100,000 and bought more than 150 protective canine vests. Now these police dogs are as safe as their human partners.

Jane Smith, Michael Carter's teacher, taught a very important lesson about caring.

Caring people feel for others. They listen to and support the people around them. But caring people also take action. They work to help people in need. Here is how one person made a difference by turning caring into action.

In August 1999 schoolteacher Jane Smith of Fayetteville, North Carolina, learned that one of her middle school students needed a new kidney. A kidney is an organ in the body that filters wastes and other impurities from the blood. People are born with two kidneys.

The student was Michael Carter. Michael had suffered from kidney disease since he was a toddler. Because of the disease, one of his kidneys did not develop properly. Then when Michael was 13, his second kidney began to fail.

Some of Michael's family and friends wanted to donate a kidney to him. However, to donate a kidney, the donor must have blood and tissue types that match those of the person getting the organ. None of Michael's relatives or friends were a match.

Smith offered to donate one of her kidneys to Michael. After testing her blood and tissue types, doctors learned that she and Michael were a match.

On April 14, 2000, doctors removed Smith's left kidney. The same day, they transplanted the kidney into Michael's body. The operation was a success, and Michael returned to school a few months later. Today Michael is doing well, thanks to a teacher who cared.

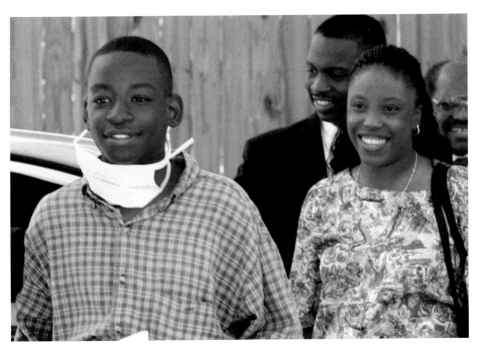

Michael Carter, left, and his mother, Deborah Evans, right, leave UNC Hospitals five days after he received a kidney from his middle school teacher, Jane Smith. Evans says that Smith is her son's "guardian angel."

A native of the Dominican Republic, Sammy Sosa gained fame and fans as a heavy hitter for the Chicago Cubs.

Sammy Sosa is best known for his ability to belt a baseball out of the park. As right fielder for the Chicago Cubs, he has won games and broken records. He was even voted Major League Baseball's Most Valuable Player. But many of Sosa's most lasting achievements have taken place off the field. He is a great example of a famous person who shows that he cares about others.

Despite his superstar status, Sosa has never forgotten his humble beginnings. Sosa grew up in the Dominican Republic, an island nation in the Caribbean. His family was so poor that he could not afford a baseball glove. Instead he made a glove out of an old milk carton.

Once Sosa became a heavy hitter in the United States, he wanted to do something good with the money that he was earning. He decided to help poor children back in the Dominican Republic get a good start in life. The baseball player donated money and computers to Dominican schools. He also founded a medical center in his hometown of San Pedro de Macoris. Children receive some free health care at the center.

Sosa also shows that he cares about his homeland in times of trouble. In 1998 when Hurricane Georges slammed into the Dominican Republic, Sosa sprang into action. He helped raise thousands of dollars in aid and supplies for the Dominican people. When it comes to caring, Sammy Sosa hits a grand slam!

This boy lives in Sammy Sosa's hometown of San Pedro de Macoris, Dominican Republic. The Sammy Sosa Foundation contributed money for rebuilding the stadium there.

The Power of Forgiveness

One way to show caring is to forgive people who have wronged you. This is not always easy. When someone hurts you, you may feel angry. But you can show that you care about people by forgiving their bad deeds. Forgiving can also break the cycle of violence and hatred. Here are two examples of people who cared enough about others to forgive them.

Azim Khamisa's son was 20 years old when he was shot and killed in San Diego, California, in 1995. Instead of seeking vengeance, Khamisa tried to forgive the 14-year-old gang member charged with his son's murder. He contacted the boy's grandfather, and together the two worked through the

Azim Khamisa, left, reached out to Ples Felix, the grandfather of Tony Hicks, the young gang member who killed his 20-year-old son, Tariq.

terrible tragedy. The two men went into schools and talked to students about the effects of the shooting on both families. Khamisa went on to found the Tariq Khamisa Foundation in honor of his son. The foundation looks for ways to end violence.

Thomas Takashi Tanemori also believes in forgiveness. In 1945 six of Tanemori's family members were killed when the United States dropped an atomic bomb on Hiroshima, Japan, to force Japan's surrender at the end of World War II. Tanemori survived, but he

After years of being angry and bitter, Thomas Takashi Tanemori learned to forgive the people who hurt his family.

was filled with anger. He traveled to the United States, hoping to find a better life. Over the years, Tanemori realized that his anger was hurting himself and those that he loved. Today Tanemori talks to others about peace and forgiveness to show that he cares.

In 1995, 12-year-old Craig Kielburger of Toronto, Canada, read a story that changed his life. The story was about a boy who was murdered in Pakistan because he spoke out against child labor. After reading the story, the Canadian youth decided to do what he could to make the world a more caring place for kids.

Craig and a group of friends founded Free the Children. Free the Children is an international group that works to help children everywhere. Free the Children focuses on children's rights, child labor, poverty, and many other issues that affect kids.

Free the Children has been successful in helping kids around the world. Group members have helped build 300 schools, numerous health centers, and two children's centers. The group has also distributed millions of dollars worth of medical supplies and school kits. Today Free the

Small Act of Caring

Make a list of five things that you can do to make the world around you a kinder, more caring place.

Craig Kielburger founded Free the Children in 1996, when he was 13 years old. Free the Children was formed to fight for children's rights.

Children is the largest organization for kids helping kids in the world. More than 100,000 kids from 35 different nations are members.

Craig keeps a busy schedule. He travels around the world, speaking with teens and others about his cause. He hopes to encourage and inspire people to become compassionate and caring leaders.

Civil rights movement: The struggle by black Americans to gain equality

Compassion: A desire to ease the troubles of others.

Empathy: The ability to put yourself into another person's place.

Forgiveness: The act of forgiving someone for a wrong that they have done.

Peer mediator: A student who is specially trained to help other students work out conflicts and problems.

Canfield, Jack. *Chicken Soup for the Kid's Soul.* Deerfield
   Beach, Florida: Health Communications, Inc., 1998.
   Here are 101 stories for kids about caring, courage,
and kindness.

Markova, Dawna. *Kids' Random Acts of Kindness.* Berkeley,
   California: Conari Press, 1994.
   This book contains stories by and for kids that
demonstrate acts of caring and kindness.

Mikaelson, Ben. *Touching Spirit Bear.* New York:
   HarperCollins Publishers, 2001.
   This work of fiction tells the story of a teen who turns
away from anger and violence and learns the power of
forgiveness and caring.

www.amazing-kids.org
   This "amazing" web site celebrates the achievements
of caring kids.